Wirral vikings:

The Wider Context

Hrolf Douglasson

First Published 2005 by Countyvise Limited,
14 Appin Road, Birkenhead, Wirral CH41 9HH.

Copyright © 2005 Hrolf Douglasson

The right of Hrolf Douglasson to be identified as the author of this work has been asserted by him in accordance with the Copyright, Design and Patents Act 1988.

British Library Cataloguing in Publication Data.
A catalogue record for this book is available from the British Library.

Please note: From 1st January 2007 ISBNs will contain 13 numbers these numbers will be the same as the present number printed below the barcode (ie. starting 978).
Countyvise is showing both existing (10 digit) and future (13 digit) ISBNs on the Title page verso. Please continue to use the 10 figure number until 31st December 2006.

ISBN 1 901231 57 7   ISBN 978 1 901231 57 1

Cover Photograph: Courtesy of J.K. Siddorn & Regia Anglorum

DEDICATION

This book is dedicated to my wife, Elvara,
and my three children,
for all their support and help along the way.

Contents

Acknowledgements

I would like to express my thanks for help and support in the production of this book to the following:

To Mr. J. K. Siddorn, and Regia Anglorum, for permission to use the cover photograph, depicting one of the Society's replica longships under full sail.

To Mr. Antony Green, for the internal photographs. Further thanks to Mrs. P. Green for help and assistance during the long journeys between photo sessions on my behalf.

To Professor Steve Harding, for unwittingly providing part of the initial impetus to write this book in the first place. Wirhalh Skip- Felag share the blame in this, although I was also given free rein to plunder their extensive library...

Introduction

Much has been written regarding the arrival on Wirral of exiled Norsemen from Dublin at the start of the tenth century; pioneering work by Dodgson, Wainright and others down the years, beginning during the revival of Viking interest in the nineteenth century and continuing through the twentieth, has managed to flesh out the bare bones of the story, and most books dealing with Viking-Age Britain and Ireland include at least a brief summary of these events. This book sets out to place those bare bones within the body to which I believe they belong: the wider context of an "Irish Sea Culture" that flourished around the Norse-derived settlements and peoples that inhabited the coasts of that expanse of water. Events on Wirral did not happen in isolation; they occurred within this context, as part of a series of events which all helped to shape the world around Wirral between the ninth and twelfth centuries. The arrival of Dublin's exiles in 902 is but one episode examined here.

Reconstructing this wider context is not as easy a task as might be thought. Sources from the period exist, but they are scattered and somewhat sparse. They are also marked by the particular interests and biases of their compilers, and few of them are what might be considered complete. To these must be added the findings of the archaeologists, which increase year by year, but are not always available to the general reader or enthusiast for some time after the initial excavations. Placing such results and discoveries into the wider context also requires time, and again, takes us back to the contemporary sources in the hope of at least partial understanding of what was going on at the time.

As a result, a lot of this book, as with any history, must be regarded as "best guess", but such guesses are the result of long and careful study of every available source. Cross-referencing such material can throw up interesting points, and shed light into previously shadowy areas. As a consequence, this "best guess" is a solid set of ideas, built upon each other, and all backed up by documentary or archaeological evidence.

I have presented the available evidence in a way that, as far as I am aware, has not been done before. Rather than attempt a chronological narrative, bringing in various sources as they became relevant, I have chosen to gather all the sources from a particular region together, and go through them as a group, in the hope of presenting the viewpoint of the peoples contemporary to the events happening on Wirral. The final Summary is the place in which chronology once more takes over, and with the evidence from regional opinions of the Wirral Norse behind it, the timeline is somewhat more complete than would otherwise be the case.

My own interest in this subject, and the initial impetus for this book, is a direct result of my leadership for many years of the Wirral's own Viking re-enactment society, the Wirhalh Skip-Felag, who can still be found in public display all around the peninsula at every opportunity. As the only History graduate in the group, research into what we portray naturally fell within my many remits, and I was happy to oblige. This book is one of the results. I have since moved away from Wirral, but retain my interest in an area that has seen a surprising amount of action over the centuries, and whose hills and fields hold many secrets yet to be unlocked.

The English
Evidence

The Anglo-Saxon Chronicles first make mention of the Wirral in an entry for the year 893, when a "Danish" army based in Essex secured their headquarters, containing women and ships, and then "…went in one stretch, by day and night, till they came to an empty town in the Wirral, which is called Chester"[1]. The entry for the following year describes how, deprived of food resources by a besieging force of West Saxons, the Danes broke out into North Wales before turning back towards Essex, via Northumbria and East Anglia.

The full story may well be a little more complex, and this episode merely serves to illustrate how sparse the entries in the Chronicles can be. There is no reason given for the Danish army's breakout from what was arguably a secure and well-defended winter haven; they had, according to the Chronicle, only just reached it after fleeing from a seemingly disastrous campaign and battle in the south-west. Possibly it began as a diversionary tactic; it is possible to read a concern for their women and offspring into the surviving records of Viking military activities across most of Europe, if one cares to look for it[2]. The subsequent march from one side of England to the other seems to serve no clear military purpose either, other than an implied desire to out-run a postulated force of pursuing Saxons. The Chronicle's only comment is that, once within Chester, "…the army could not come up behind them…"[3], which could be construed either as a pursuing force out of Essex, or another detachment heading up from the site of the recent English victory, i.e., Devon. Given what is known of English military structure at this time, however, the likelihood of a

THE ROUTE OF DANISH AND WESSEX ARMIES 893 A.D.

single, coherent army chasing Vikings from east to west and then back again is minimal. Anglo-Saxon armies were short-term, temporary affairs for the most part. Whilst the "greater fyrd" contained the nobility and their sons and hangers-on of the district, and was the closest to a standing army the English had, the more numerous "lesser fyrd" was composed of local freemen and farmers, whose term of service was limited to around three months at most, but more importantly, their sphere of operations was strictly limited to their home county, or its ruling eorldom[4]. So the fyrd that chased the Danish force out of Essex would have stopped at the border, or more likely at the next big settlement they came across, where the next local authority could be appraised of the situation and his own troops gathered. If the eorl was good at his job, he might send runners ahead with the news that the Danes were on the move, hoping to catch them between his own forces and those ahead. In such forward planning lay a greater chance, if not of victory, then at least of survival for the majority of his men.

From south to north, however, the situation in 893 was different. These Vikings had been forcibly driven out of Devon, the heart of Wessex; now they were heading north into Mercia. In theory separate kingdoms, as indeed were Essex and East Anglia, in practice Mercia was tied to the House of Wessex by marriage. Not only did the shadow of Alfred "the Great" loom over his northerly neighbour (although there is debate about exactly when this particular epithet was first coined, it is fairly safe to assume that his reputation was already well-known beyond his borders), but his daughter, Aethelflaed, was wife to the Mercian king Aethelred - and he was not in the best of health, as we shall see in due course. So if armies were able to move between kingdoms in pursuit of Danish opponents, the greater likelihood is that they were coming from Wessex, into Mercia, with at least royal acceptance, if not outright approval.

The Chronicles are not specific about how long it actually took this particular force of Vikings to get to their destination either, and the calculation is made more difficult by lack of information as to the exact route, and the mode of transportation used. Suffice to say that, even using modern motorways and modern vehicles, a journey from Chester to Norfolk takes around nine hours, so it is not unreasonable to allow the best part of a week or more for an army mostly walking to make the trip. Not having any clear idea about the numerical size of the army, we cannot say whether or not they might all have been mounted.

But, given the apparent security of the base, and the state of the army within it, why go in the first place? The Chronicles specify that Chester at this time is deserted, and imply that Wirral is equally so. Stenton, however, observes that Chester would have made a good base for raiding into Mercia, and also that "...reinforcement from the Scandinavian settlements in Ireland was possible"[5]. It is unlikely, however, that any Viking leader worth his salt would ever have undertaken such a march unless he was sure of his reception at the other end; presumably the Danes expected easy pickings in Mercia, or perhaps they were aware of Wirral and Chester as an area of Norse activity already. As we shall see shortly, the presence of Norse settlers in Wirral is usually only pinned down to the year 902 because that is when the Irish annals describe the event. Yet there is a good body of material evidence, in the form of chance finds over some two hundred years or more, that suggests large areas of the north-west of England, including Lancashire and Cumbria, were already home or seasonal base to people of Norwegian or Danish ancestry[6]. There is nothing, of course, to say that a friendly reception around Chester and the prospect of looting the nearby Mercians need be mutually exclusive, and a chance to build up both manpower and silver, and thus reputation, must have seemed almost irresistible to any leader of a force recently mauled at the hands of the English.

That Norwegians based in Ireland were aware of Wirral as a landing place, and possibly as a gateway into Mercia, could perhaps be taken for granted. The Longphort that later became Dublin is generally thought to have been founded around 840, and raids into Anglesey and the North Welsh coasts are recorded from around the same time onwards. Only the width of the river Dee separates Wales from Wirral, and it would be churlish to suppose that any Viking ship-captain cruising into the mouth of the Dee would only have looked to the Welsh side of his vessel. Indeed, no matter which way he looked, he would be seeing Mercia, which at that time still followed the line drawn by Offas' Dyke, and thus put most of the North Welsh shore within English jurisdiction.

The surviving Chronicles that mention Mercian affairs are, sadly, all second-hand versions, and it is generally held that they all draw to varying extents on an original, now lost, Mercian Chronicle[7]. What relevant material they do contain really only begins at the year 910, and so for the pivotal events of c.902, we will have to turn elsewhere in due course. It is worth noting here, however, that the Dane's march across England occurs only nine years before the Irish and Welsh both record more definite movement into Wirral from Dublin, and this by itself is strongly suggestive of a Norse presence in the area before either the Irish or the Welsh thought it worthy of recording. The surviving Anglo-Saxon Chronicles are silent of events in Mercia for 902; in 903 the dedication of a new church in Chester is mentioned, which may seem strange for a city described as deserted only ten years before. In 907, "Chester was restored"[8]; in 911, more notice is taken, chiefly because of the death of Aethelred, described in the Chronicles as "Lord of Mercia", or sometimes as "Eorldorman of Mercia", but in theory at least, an independent king of an independent Mercia. In the ordinary way of things, one king would be replaced by another, subject to the approval of the local Witan, a body roughly analogous to the House of Lords, but with the power to dethrone a king they did not want by simply refusing to recognise him. On this occasion, however, there was no new king; instead, his wife, Aethelflaed, described in loving terms as "The Lady of the Mercians" by the Chroniclers, set about ruling Mercia in her own right, and was soon communicating with her brother Edward, king of East Anglia (if not of Wessex too, on the death of his father), with regard to a proposed major, joint offensive against the Danish-controlled areas in the east of England. Aethelflaed and Edward were the offspring of Alfred, who, in recognising the power of the Danes over large areas of the country and agreeing to a partition of England, had bought his successors time to regroup, refinance, and form a plan of action aimed at the re-integration of the Danelaw into a greater Wessex. It may be that the incursion of 893 had triggered the dormant enmity of Alfred's progeny towards the incomers into definite action; it may also be that the presence of Aethelred as titular king of Mercia had acted as a brake on such feelings, and prevented any effective diversion of scarce resources towards military endeavours conducted largely outside his own realm. We have already noticed that the intrusions into Mercia of 893 may well have been resisted by troops from Wessex, which does tend to suggest an inability on the part of the Mercians to deal with such threats, be that inability financial or otherwise. Whatever the reasons behind the delay in taking action, once Aethelred was dead, things began to happen. Edward gained London and Oxford, which until then had presumably been counted as either Mercian or part of Wessex; in 912, both he and his sister were engaged in the building of multiple Burghs, fortified townships developed by their father within Wessex, and now spreading northwards. The following year, Aethelflaed is credited with the building of no less than four large royal Burghs across her kingdom. The pattern was set; from this time on, if one accepts the Chronicle versions as accurate, the English were always victorious against the "Danes", towns were captured, and forts built. By 917, Aethelflaed had Derby in her grasp; the next year, Leicester. York, the Northumbrian capital, had entered into negotiations with her, and in theory put itself under her rule, but before the deal could be finalised, the Lady of the Mercians died, leaving her brother Edward commanding, not only his own people, but those of Northumbria and Mercia as well. By way of demonstration, he commanded the building of a Burgh at Thelwall, in Cheshire, and refortified Manchester, manning it with a mixed force of Mercians and Northumbrians. More or less as a footnote, the Chronicle also records that Aethelflaed's daughter, named as Aelfwynn, "...was deprived of all power in Mercia, and taken into Wessex..."[9]. Did she perhaps take after her father, and prefer to concentrate on rebuilding the Mercian infrastructure? By this date, such an attitude would have been highly inconvenient to her uncle, and it is hard to see who else was in any position to displace her.

Whatever Edward was hoping to achieve in Mercia, his efforts there only helped Northumbria slip from his grasp; in that same year, 919, the Northumbrians, ever eager for a way out of English control, took one Raegnold, or Ragnald, for their king. From the form of his name, it could be surmised that Ragnald was no Englishman, and hindsight could suggest that this was when something of a tradition began in Northumbria: the reneging on a promise of loyalty to any given English king, distant in Wessex, in favour of an incoming Scandinavian hopeful on the doorstep. Kings travelled with large and well-armed retinues during this period, and for the nobility of York, discretion may often have seemed the better part of valour. It did them little good, for in 920, the Chronicle records Ragnald, and a host of others, paying homage and fealty to Edward. Not recorded by the Chronicle, however, but found in other English and foreign sources, is an invasion across the Cheshire plains from Dublin in this same year, showing that Edward's efforts at Thelwall had been with good reason[10]. With fortresses at Thelwall, Runcorn, Chester and, from recent discoveries, probably Rhuddlan (now in North Wales) as well, Edward and Aethelflaed had effectively surrounded the Norse on the Wirral, and place-names on the peninsula show a clear line of demarcation between Scandinavian and Englishman[11].

With the passing of Aethelflaed, Mercia fades back into obscurity in the English records, appearing only vaguely, and usually in times of trouble or unrest. King Edward was at Chester in 924, apparently dealing with an uprising concocted between the men of Chester, and the Welsh. No further details survive, but one cannot help but wonder what the men of Wirral were doing at the time. In 936 or 7 (there is continuing uncertainty about the precise date, and the Welsh place it in 938), Edward's successor Aethelstan, who incidentally was reared at the Mercian court of Aethelred and Aethelflaed, is recorded as fighting and winning a decisive battle over a combined force of Strathclydesmen, Welsh, and Dubliners, at a now-lost location called Brunnanburh. Research by members of the English Place-Name Society, along with a number of local traditions, places Brunnanburh at modern Bromborough, on the Mersey side of the Wirral. The argument is a strong one, on a number of counts; geographically, the lie of the land resembles that described in the poem commemorating the victory, whilst strategically, the easiest way to gather a force from lowland Scotland, Ireland and Wales would be by sea, and Bromborough has always had a good, sheltered anchorage. Once assembled, the invader's plan was probably to march on York (a theme to be replayed over and over by kings of Dublin), and re-establish Northumbria as an independent kingdom (Aethelstan had annexed it almost as soon as he was crowned), to form an axis of power from Dublin in the west to Nidaros (modern Trondheim) in the east. It came to nothing; the Wessex king was a good warrior, as kings had to be, and the incoming army never even made it to Chester before Aethelstan seemingly caught them by surprise, and, if the Chronicle poetry (amazingly the only known record of what must have

THE ROUTES TO BRUANBURGH

been a pivotal point in the history of England), is reliable, annihilated them. And broadly accurate it has to be, for subsequent events would have been vastly different had the invaders won the day; for one thing, we would probably have no knowledge of Athelstan, the line of Wessex kings could have looked vastly different, at least until the rise of Harold Godwinsson, and Northumbria may well have been a stronger power, bolstered by Dublin, for a lot longer than it was. There were survivors from the losing coalition; they took to their ships, and made for Dublin, a factor in the account that supporters of inland or east-coast locations for Brunnanburh have never been able to reconcile, but something that could hardly be easier from a west-coast base[12].

Perhaps surprisingly, whilst Wirral as a distinct entity is not mentioned in the main English sources, beyond the entry for 893 noted at the beginning of this chapter, Chester is only slightly more prominent. In 893, it was described as "in the Wirral"; whether this geographical nicety was still recognised almost a century later is unknown. Even if it was, to judge by the place-name evidence it was well beyond the Norse-English frontier zone, safely within Mercian cultural and political territory, and thus a part of the new England. In 973, his coronation year, three of the Chronicle manuscripts record that King Edgar came to Chester, and there received the submission of six tributary kings. Later versions add more and more detail into this bald account, naming these kings, and asserting that their homage took the form of rowing Edgar upon the Dee; but these are all details added long after the events, and whilst not impossible (except perhaps for some of the names, which have been impossible to trace), they should perhaps be treated with due caution[13]. Chester also then disappears until the years after the Conquest, so that without the help of archaeological evidence, we should hardly even know it was there. Coin hoards uncovered in the city and its environs suggest periods of unrest and uncertainty for at least some of the residents: of the four discovered (all now, sadly, incomplete and three not very well recorded either), one has a postulated date of around 917, whilst the others lie between 960 and 980. According to the Chronicle, 917 was a violent year, with a great amount of troop movement and action being detailed: but it all happens in the east of England, around Cambridgeshire and Huntingdon. The closest action to Chester is Aethelflaed's taking of Derby. Westmorland was "ravaged" in 966, by one Thored Gunnarsson, whilst, as we have just seen, Edgar was part of some significant ceremonial in Chester in 973. In 978, Aethelred, soon to be known as "Unraed", came to the English throne in less than ideal circumstances (his half-brother having been murdered, almost certainly on the orders of his mother), but how long it took for this news to have any real effect on popular thinking is impossible to say. According to the Chronicle, his coronation was accompanied by unnatural phenomena that may have had more relevance for the man in the street. Cheshire is again recorded as being attacked in 980, but this is a brief entry in the most vague of terms, and tells us little beyond a general confirmation that these were, indeed, troubled times.

No matter how troubled (or troubling) Wirral and Chester may have been, there is some slight evidence that the king did not entirely desert them. An entry for 1000 suggests that Chester was a royal ship-base; however, after failing to meet their master as he ravaged Cumberland, they set off and attacked the Isle of Man instead[14]. Were these ships perhaps more Wirral than Chester in their parentage? Or is there, in this entry, the beginnings of the Chronicle compiler's marked antipathy towards Aethelred? It is unlikely, given the rest of the Chronicle material to compare it with, that any of the scribes writing the entries had more than the most garbled and untrustworthy reports of any incidents from so far north. Aethelred ended his life in illness; in 1016, the year of his death, Edmund Ironside ravaged Chester as part of his ongoing campaign against Cnut - the city had refused to levy troops for his fight against the Dane - but before the year was out, he and Cnut had divided England between them, and Cnut got Mercia, which may possibly indicate a division along broadly ethnic lines. Not that it mattered in the long run: Edmund was dead within the year, and Cnut reigned England alone.

There was a tradition that a wooden bench sited at Leasowe on Wirral was the chair on which Cnut famously attempted to turn back the waves. The seat no longer exists, although photographs remain, and they do not show an eleventh-century style in any way. Furthermore, the timber is in far too good a state of preservation for it to have been genuine, and so this legend can be discounted. It is not impossible that Cnut came to Wirral, or, more likely, Chester, during his reign, but how warm a welcome a

Danish warlord would get from a fiercely independent colony of largely Norwegian extraction is debatable. In Ireland, Danes and Norwegians were often on opposing sides. But Chester had defied Edmund's request for troops, and so Cnut may have felt on firm enough ground to visit.

From this time on, the Chronicle becomes less of a recording of momentous events, and more of a political commentary, as it charts almost to the exclusion of all else, the rise of the house of Godwin. Place-names become scarce; details are glossed over or omitted altogether, while the names of the key players appear over and over again. Chester is named as the base for an Irish ship-force raised by the outlawed eorl Aelfgar Leofricsson, once he had been re-instated to Mercia after burning Hertford and its inhabitants in pursuit of his case. He was outlawed again in 1058, and this time employed Norwegian ships to get back in - "it is long to tell how it all happened"[15]. And, sadly, the Chronicle considers it too long to be worthwhile.

In the early days of 1063, Harold Godwinsson attacked Rhuddlan, now in the hands of Gruffydd of Gwynedd, and he appears to have proceeded from Gloucester, via Chester, rather than try and force a passage through mid-Wales in the middle of winter. One assumes that Chester was friendly towards him, as no mention is made of punitive action towards the town. This assumption no longer holds true by 1069, when fragmentary evidence, generally thought to be older than the extant Chronicles, suggests that Cheshire was included in William's punitive expedition against northern rebellion and unrest, that also saw York burnt to the ground[16].

There is a final reference to our area of interest within the English source material, but from the Chronicle, one could easily overlook it. In 1098, we are told "Eorl Hugo was killed in Anglesey by sea-rovers..."[17]. We will have to turn to the Welsh, the Irish, and particularly the Norwegian sources, to flesh out the bones of this tale, and a suitably spectacular finale it turns out to be.

CONCLUSIONS

Having trawled the available English primary sources, and then turned to respected secondary ones for further inspiration, it is hard not to come away with the conviction that North-West England mattered little to those whose duty was to record the momentous events of the years. Tucked away in relatively sheltered cloisters well within the heartlands of Wessex and later England (although it should be remembered that nowhere was particularly "safe" in the modern, universal, sense: many monasteries suffered plagues, starvation and neglect even if they were not the subjects of actual physical attack), Chester must have seemed a world away, a mere name on a page. Wirral, without even the mental image of a walled town to accompany it, can at best have been considered the edge of that world, an area of wilderness without towns, roads, or information. The Roman empire, which organised things differently and paid more attention to good communication lines over long distances, was well aware of Wirral, as archaeology has shown: the peninsula can boast at least one good road, and a supply farm for the garrison in Deva (Chester), sited at Irby. Similar remains are found along the Welsh coast, notably at Prestatyn, and so it can be inferred that, in Roman times, Wirral was a fully-integrated section of Britannia Minor Province. It has yet to be demonstrated whether Chester hosted any of the Germanic auxilliary units now thought to have been moved into Britain some time before the final withdrawal in the fifth century, and it has further yet to be proved that any such units, or part thereof, remained behind when the legions proper were withdrawn and Rome retreated into its own internal power-struggles. What is beyond reasonable doubt is that, by the end of the ninth century, Wirral and west Cheshire were a self-contained, politically and geographically isolated corner of an island divided into four or five separate kingdoms, who all looked inwards towards each other, at the expense of peripheries and neighbours.

This tendency to look inwards was one of the factors that made the initial Viking raids of the eighth century so devastating: reading what was written at the time, one is struck by the sense of utter surprise with which they happened. The English never saw them coming, and once aware of them, the Chronicle in particular takes great pains to track the movements of the various "forces" around the well-known areas of middle England, as if losing sight of them for an instant might bring further havoc and ruin. But on the coasts, when away from population centres, the information is more vague, less precise. Is it into this "somehow less important" category of geography that the Anglo-Saxon writers place Wirral and its environs. The Irish and the Welsh viewed it with rather more immediacy, as events around Wirral often impacted more upon their own territories, and it is to them that we now turn for more detailed information.

NOTES

[1]   The Anglo-Saxon Chronicles, ed. Anne Savage, Guild, 1986
[2]   Judith Jesch, " Women In The Viking Age", Boydell, 2003
[3]   Savage, 1986
[4]   Frank Stenton, "Anglo-Saxon England", Oxford, 1988
[5]   ibid.
[6]   A good introduction to this material, though not exhaustive, is Edwards,"Vikings in North West England, CNWRS (Lancaster), 1998
[7]   Savage, 1986
[8]   ibid.
[9]   ibid.
[10] Hunter-Blair,1974, pp83-4
[11] Cavill, Harding, Jesch: "Wirral and its Viking Heritage", EPNS, Nottingham, 2000
[12] ibid. See also Harding's inspired solution to the problems posed by "Dingesmere" (forthcoming as of 2004)
[13] Stenton, 1988
[14] Savage, 1986
[15] ibid.
[16] Stenton, 1988
[17] Savage, 1986

The Evidence
from Chester

Over the last fifty years or so, large areas of the city of Chester have become available for excavation by archaeologists, usually as a result of ongoing urban redevelopment within the city walls. Areas to both sides of the present Northgate Street have been investigated, along with sections of Watergate Street, Pepper Street and Lower Bridge Street. Whilst the main thrust of many such digs was directed at recovering more evidence of the Roman phases of occupation, later levels have not been ignored, and in some areas it has been possible to construct a model of Anglo-Saxon occupation and site usage, especially for the era when Chester was "restored" in the words of the Anglo-Saxon Chronicles: in other words, in precisely the time zone we are interested in, the time when Aethelflaed refortified the town against attacks from her new Viking neighbours.

It became very obvious from a number of excavations around the city centre that the Anglo-Saxon street plan was often influenced by the remains of the Roman fortress and street layout. In areas where substantial buildings still existed, the new owners built around or within their walls, and adapted their living arrangements to suit; however, where the Roman structures had already collapsed, notably along areas of the fortress wall, new alignments appeared, seemingly based mainly on lines of easier excavation for foundations. Indeed, none of this should come as too much of a surprise, when it is discovered that one of the monks of the Abbey, one Ranulph Higden, wrote in the fourteenth century that much of the Roman city was still visible and, indeed, usable[1]. Certainly the alignment of the four roads out of the city that follow the cardinal compass points are known to have utilised the remains of the Roman gateways, and were even slightly realigned in the early Middle Ages to deal with the partial blockage of some of the portals[2]. Overall, it appears that when the Danish army referred to in previous chapters reached that "deserted" city of Chester, what they actually found was a defensible and occupied Roman survival, with its walls and buildings largely intact. The status of the population at this time is uncertain, as those areas excavated both within and outside the Roman walls seem to have been largely given over to agriculture; having said this, of course, it remains that somebody must have been resident in order to be ploughing. The bottom-most levels investigated at Lower Bridge Street suggest multiple users, as regular strips of ploughed land were divided by parallel ditches[3]. The pursuing English only maintained their attempts at a siege for two or three days; either their term of duty expired, or, more likely, they took one look at the fortress, considered the reputation of its new inhabitants, and decided to cut their losses. Had the residents outside the walls been friendly, they might have stayed longer or fared better, which raises the likelihood that even at this early stage, Chester had strong links with local Scandinavians operating in the Irish Sea area.

Within a very short space of time after the events of 902-907, whatever arguments existed between Mercia and Viking Wirral had been resolved, and archaeology shows a picture of a healthy, indeed prospering, Norse element in Chester's population, and not just in the region now occupied by Lower Bridge Street, which has been considered as something of a Viking "cultural Quarter" by many researchers. However, this profitable section of land lay outside the walls of the original Roman fortress, a point which may have some bearing on the apparent decision to extend the defences in the south and west, and thus bring this area within the confines of the new burgh[4]. Little evidence survives of Anglo-Saxon defensive gates at any site - Tamworth is the notable exception - and the image of huge wooden doors that could be closed against the enemy dates from a later time. Saxon defences at gateways may have relied more on Roman leftovers where these were available, or a number of burly men with spears to plug the gaps. Certainly the extensions at Chester had the advantage of being straightforward sections, probably a ditch, rampart and palisade in the initial phases, without the need for new gateways, as these already existed. The new walls also took the burgh area right down to the river on two of its four sides, which served a number of useful functions. Firstly, it facilitated trade with the outside world; secondly, it provided a ready-made defence along those two sides, with a second line of defence provided by the remaining Roman wall; thirdly, it brought wealthy, money-generating sections of the population within the boundaries of the tax-gathering royal establishment. The new scheme thus provided an "inner city", surrounded by the original Roman defences, and a new "outer city", where new development could be planned, industry established, and potential undesirables or transients housed.

Chester flourished; its Norse component flourished with it. Coins are a well-attested method of judging the inherent wealth of any city in this period, and coins from a Chester mint have been found far beyond its immediate vicinity. No less than twenty-six different individuals have been identified as moneyers from the city, suggesting that a huge amount of silver was passing through the town over a considerable period of time. In the reign of Athelstan, Chester is believed to have been the largest mint in England; sadly, the situation did not endure, as by the time of Aethelred II "Unraed", the boom appears to have been over. A large Viking incursion into Cheshire around 980 may have tipped an already fragile economy over the edge for Chester; if the city's wealth and influence were in any part due to the activities of friendly, integrated Anglo-Scandinavians, the reappearance of serious numbers of destructive semi-cousins in the region would not have done a lot for investor confidence. Excavations around the Northgate area of the city suggest buildings were abandoned, possibly even deliberately burned down, around this period, and the rubble was just left to the elements instead of being cleared and the land reused. Similarly, an impressive urban development in the vicinity of Lower Bridge Street appears to have been dismantled at this time, and the site abandoned[5]. It is possible, given his generally anti-foreigner stance, that Aethelred Unraed did not care for a city so full of non-English as Chester appears to have been, and his successor Edmund attacked the city in retaliation for its refusal to raise an army against Svein Forkbeard and his son Cnut in 1016. All these factors, coupled with the gradual rise of Bristol (deep in the heart of Wessex) as an alternative trading gateway to Ireland at the same time, combined to end Chester's brief period as perhaps the foremost settlement in the country. By the time of the Conquest, there appears to have been little in the way to prevent large-scale reorganisations of the inner-city streets that accommodated the new Minster and castle, and paid little heed to what had gone before.

When the Danish army of 893 arrived in Chester, they came to a city that was as much Welsh as English or Norse: the Mercians had only won it in recent times, before which it had counted as eastern Powys. Archaeology suggests that much of the city was being used for agriculture of various sorts (one surviving Roman building appears to have been used as a cattle pen[6]), a usage that only changes to urban habitation, and traces of industrial activity, around the time of Aethelflaed's restoration of the burgh, as noted above. The soils previously built up are replaced by post-holes, and the sunken trenches of grubenhausen. It is clear that the new activity was still often influenced by the echoes of Rome, for trenches and pits are often dug in the easier sections of ground: the alleys between barrack-blocks, for example, or bitten into the edges of roads. Where stone was available above ground, or just below the surface, it often shows signs of cursory robbing, as if the new builders only took what they needed rather than attempting to clear an entire site. Where the footings of buildings had vanished under the soil, they were built over, usually on new alignments that presumably reflect new roads and streets being laid out.

One feature that appears to have been renewed, however, is the roadway around the inside of the fortress wall. It could not follow the precise line of its Roman predecessor due to alterations in the structure of the walls themselves: the loss of most, if not all, of the original interval towers, and the reuse of at least one partially collapsed section that had been converted into a row of ovens. Nonetheless, its presence at all in the new Saxon burgh suggests that the walls were still largely intact, and that the concept of an encircling street was familiar from other sites, both Roman and Anglo-Saxon. From this, we can conclude that Aethelflaed and her architects were following established practice; that is to say, Chester was the latest in a series of similar remodellings around the country, and nor would it be the last. Furthermore, at this time burghs were a Wessex phenomenon, which as noted elsewhere, points to more than just a marriage between Mercia and the family of Alfred. Burghs were to become the tool by which Aethelflaed and her brother Edward would regain much of the Danelaw for Wessex; Chester's inclusion within this scheme helps put its many alterations and changes into this wider context.

NOTES

[1]   Polychronicon, Higden; ed. Babington, 1869.

[2]   Excavations At Chester (report 7: Saxon Occupation Within The Roman Fortress), Ward et al, Chester 1994. It should also be noted, however, that in the area now occupied by the bus station and adjacent Market Hall, the Roman plan appears to have been largely abandoned. The reasons for this are not entirely clear, as the surviving remains from this period are still quite substantial, and one would expect them to have had more influence than is the case.

[3]   Excavations At Chester (report 3: 26-42 Lower Bridge Street 1974-6; the Dark Age and Saxon Periods), Mason, Chester, 1985.

[4]   ibid.

[5]   For Northgate, see Ward; for Lower Bridge Street, see Mason. The overall picture from Chester towards the end of the tenth century is one of sudden, rapid decline and abandonment across the city. This is too extreme a phenomenon to be ascribed entirely to short-term traumas such as renewed Viking activity.

[6]   Ward, p.116

The Welsh
Evidence

Until comparatively recently, little work had been attempted on the evidence for Norse activity around the Principality: the sources are mostly late compilations of earlier, lost, originals, and contain a great deal of material that is difficult to interpret, or is garbled versions of unrelated texts, or is just plain fantasy, or any combination of these. What roughly contemporary sources there are, are terse and brief in the extreme, giving the historian a choice of extremes from which to choose! Within it all, however, there is still some useful historical recording, and when coupled to place-name evidence and recent advances in archaeology, a much clearer and more detailed picture begins to emerge.

The "Annales Cambriae", or Welsh Annals, comprise a list of events, dated year by year, covering the period from AD444 (although it is generally considered that the list was intended to begin at 447, and most modern editions of the list make this correction)[1], to 977. Unlike the Anglo-Saxon Chronicles, however, the entries are minimalist, just the briefest of notes regarding what were considered relevant or important events and people, and so it is hard to imagine just what intended use lay behind the compiling of the Annals in the first place.

Its use in illuminating events in the Wirral and Chester is therefore limited, but it is another piece in our jigsaw. It records a battle at Chester in 613, and notes various happenings and deaths among "the Saxons", i.e., people not Welsh (or "British"). It confirms the first appearance of Norsemen in Ireland under the year 796, and, the following year, a battle

INGIMUND'S JOURNEY

at Rhuddlan, just inland from the southern shore of the Dee. The entry is ambiguous, but this may have been fought between the English Mercians and their Welsh neighbours, for at this time Offa's Dyke was still an effective frontier, and Rhuddlan was only just on the Welsh side of it[2].

Things hot up in the mid-ninth century. The entry for 850 says, "Cynin is killed by the gentiles"[3], and here it shows a debt to the Irish sources, in which "gentiles" is a regular substitute for "norsemen". This overseas influence in the composition is seen again in 853, when the Irish distinction between "black foreigners" and "white foreigners" is copied - the darker variety lay waste to "Mona" (Anglesey). The Mercians were deeper in enemy territory by 880, if not earlier, for in that year they fought, and seemingly lost, a battle at Conwy; the Annals describe it as "vengeance for Rhodri at God's hand"[4].

The Annals make an entry for 902 that allows us to forgive their brevity and lack of detail, for without this single sentence, our knowledge of what occurred in Wirral would be much the poorer. In this year, "Igmund came to Mona and took Maes Osfeilion"[5]. Someone called Oter is recorded as arriving in Britain during 913, and the Annals confirm Aethelflaed's death (incidentally calling her "Queen", which the English sources never do) in 917. They even confirm the battle of Brunanburgh under 938 (although this differs from the more generally accepted date of 936), and also Athelstan's death in 941.

From here on, if we want further details, we have to turn to other methods of extraction. If "Igmund", who is almost certainly the Ingimund of the Irish sources, came to Anglesey in 902, does "Maes Osfeilion" lie on the island, or elsewhere? As luck would have it, a number of Viking-Age remains have been unearthed on Anglesey: a grave at Benllech excavated in the 1940s contained fragments of artefacts suggesting a date within this period, whilst metal-detecting at Llanbedrgoch near Red Wharf Bay led in 1992, to the identification of non-Welsh coins and Viking-style lead weights. Further investigations conducted by Mark Redknap for the National Museum of Wales revealed a fortified enclosure that contained distinctly Scandinavian-styled buildings, large amounts of Hiberno-Norse styled artefacts...and a group of skeletons buried in the outer ditch, or rather, thrown in and then covered over, for these burials show no signs of reverence or formality whatsoever. One appears to have been female, and another was a child; yet another appears to have had its hands tied behind its back at the time of deposition. The presence of women and children suggests these are not incoming raiders being killed by the inhabitants, but locals being killed by incoming aggressors[6].

It would be going too far to suggest that this is surely the site that Ingimund took over in 902; for one thing, there are finds that predate the events of 902, and which suggest contacts with Anglian Northumbria as far back as the seventh century, as well as evidence of rebuilding that could push the final phase of occupation well into the eleventh century. There is evidence of domestic and industrial activities, such as leatherwork, antler-work and metal processing, that could just as easily be Welsh activity rather than Norse, whilst the defensive ditch would be equally useful and prudent to whoever occupied the site. As yet, there is no evidence as to the ethnic background of the unfortunates found at the bottom of that ditch, but radiocarbon dating suggests they may well have been there before Ingimund is believed to have arrived[7]. Furthermore, the North Welsh coast was the scene of Mercian activity around the same period, as we have already seen, and so it is not impossible that the bodies represent English aggression against the inhabitants of Red Wharf Bay.

A further sign of possible Viking activity in Wales was found in the 1930s, in Flintshire, just across the Dee from Wirral. This comprised a grave lined with stone slabs, containing a skeleton, a spearhead, and a knife blade, all sadly now lost[8]. The presence of such a grave in close proximity to the line of Offa's Dyke suggests that the Nordic presence was stronger than either the English or the Welsh, for a while at least.

Conclusions are difficult to draw, but not impossible. Contemporary Welsh records attest to Norse activity along the northern coast and on or around Anglesey, a picture which has but recently been fortified by the results of archaeology. There was certainly a settlement on Anglesey prosperous enough to attract violent attention, whilst elsewhere on the island, incoming individuals were given what their own cultures considered decent burials. Others were interred elsewhere along the

North Welsh coast, which, to judge from the documentary sources, was a long-disputed border zone between the Mercian English and the Welsh. Evidently the Nordic incomers, although late on the scene, made a significant mark on both peoples. Moreover, once they were there, they stayed, and began to build a solid, independent, republic.

NOTES

[1]   John Morris (ed): Nennius: British History and The Welsh Annals. Phillimore, 1980

[2]   This statement is made following extensive investigations as to the precise course of the Dyke, but it remains possible that the Mercians claimed Rhuddlan, and it should be noted that references in the English sources to "Cledemutha" are now considered to mean Rhuddlan. Certainly Edward I felt certain enough of its English-ness to construct a massive castle on the site of the former burgh, which remains to this day.

[3]   Morris, 1980

[4]   Ibid.

[5]   Ibid.

[6]   Mark Redknap: Vikings In Wales: An Archaeological Quest. NMGW, 2000. See also Julian Richards: Blood of the Vikings, Hodder & Stoughton, 2001, which ties in recent DNA sampling studies.

[7]   Ibid.

[8]   Ibid.

The Irish
Evidence

Compared to the brevity of the Welsh primary sources, and the absence of much interest in Mercian events from the English ones, the Irish appear positively effusive on the subject of Norse incursions onto the Wirral. It is possible to corroborate all that has so far been gleaned from the geographically closer chroniclers, and indeed flesh out the account to some degree, from the Irish sources still available to us, and it is to these, bolstered by the analysis of local place names, that modern scholarship owes most of its knowledge about the Norse settlements in the region[1].

To place matters chronologically, we can note the Annals of Ulster for the year 855, recording an attack into North Wales by one Orm, an attack which may have penetrated as far as Shropshire[2], and which may also have been responsible for the naming of the cliffs at Llandudno (although there is naturally no way of proving this). This, it can be seen, coincides rather nicely with the Welsh accounts already examined. It is generally considered that there was little, if any, direct contact between the Welsh and the Irish compilers, and on that basis, events recorded by both gain in credence. However, given the apparent ease of travel for Norsemen around the Irish Sea (it is a matter of record that a ship constructed in Dublin ended up at the bottom of Roskildefjord in Denmark), this isolation need not necessarily be so; but as it happens, there is unique material in both sets of records, as well as common threads and themes, and so it is safe enough to accept that one account reinforces and confirms the other independently.

The two main sources for the pivotal events of c. 902 are the Annals of Ulster already referred to, and another document of dubious (at best) provenance, known as The Three Fragments. Originally published in 1860 in Dublin, this was a copy of a further copy made in 1643, taken from a vellum manuscript now lost. Ordinarily, such a pedigree would rule any such document out of serious academic study, were it not for the fact that, once again, its contents can largely be corroborated from other sources considered more reliable, and archaeological discoveries bolster its content still further. It records the expulsion of "Norsemen" from Dublin, under the leadership of Ingimund, and their subsequent settlement on "lands around Chester". The document then goes on to describe in perhaps suspicious detail how Ingimund hatched a plot to seize Chester, and how these attacks were repulsed. And here we have the crux of the problem with The Three Fragments: what reliable history it may contain is all wrapped up with folk-tale and the trappings of the oral storyteller's art[3].

Stripping away the fantasy elements, what are we left with? A record of Norsemen being expelled from their longphort at Dublin, then crossing the Irish Sea to attack the Welsh, before coming to an agreement with the rulers of Mercia and settling in the area around Chester. We have the name of their alleged leader, Ingimund, and that is about as far as it is academically safe to go. We have corroboration from the Annales Cambrai and the Annals of Ulster for this much, and it is unlikely in the extreme that more than one such expedition occurred in such a short space of time. The assertion that within a few years Ingimund felt strong enough to attack Chester with a view to occupation cannot be directly corroborated, although the note in the Anglo-Saxon Chronicle that "Chester was restored" under the year 907 is often taken as evidence for this, and as explored further below, the assumption is eminently reasonable. The account of the actual siege and its motivation is almost certainly pure storytelling, however, and may be a later interpolation; certainly it is unlikely that the compiler of the original manuscript was present at the secret meetings he records in such great detail, and the sequence of triple attack-counterattack, and the strategies therein, is pure oral recitation to a standard formula. It cannot be taken as history, even of the most broad definition, and must, therefore, be set aside.

This loss of Ingimund's attempt on Chester would, however, leave the question of why Aethelflaed refortified the city in or around 907, which can be demonstrated as fact by the archaeological record. Moreover, Chester was not strengthened in isolation: a whole series of sites were refurbished and fortified throughout the years of her life in Mercia. That northern Mercia felt vulnerable cannot be doubted: there were the Danes of the Danelaw to the east, and a Norse/Danish Northumbria that stretched from Carlisle to the Humber, to the north. Now, it seems, there were incoming Norse to the west as well. To an Englishman, it must have seemed a very dangerous place to be, and the minds of Mercia's ruling classes would surely have turned to preparing adequate defences very quickly indeed. It is clear both from the English accounts, and the findings of the archaeologists, that these fortifications form two distinct groups: one along the edges of the original Danelaw, the other guarding the routes into Mercia along both the Mersey and the Dee. Whether he got the facts right or not, the point remains that the original compiler of the record now only known from The Three Fragments must have been aware of Chester's refortification, and the ultimate reason for it: the danger posed by the incoming Norsemen to Wirral and the Cheshire Plain[4].

Alongside the Annals of Ulster and The Three Fragments, another Irish compilation should be mentioned. Although not directly dealing with our main subject here, i.e. the colonisation of Wirral by Norsemen, The War Of The Irish And The Foreigners (otherwise known as the Annals of the Four Masters) remains important for its illustration of just how precise in certain respects the Irish chroniclers could be. Not surprisingly from its title, the book deals with the incursions of Nordic invaders into Ireland, and has been the source of a number of well-known quotations:

"In a word, although there were an hundred hard-steeled iron heads on one neck, and an hundred sharp, ready, never-rusting brazen tongues in every head, and an hundred garrulous, loud, unceasing voices from every tongue, they could not recount nor narrate nor enumerate nor tell what all the people of Ireland suffered in common, both men and women, laymen and priests, old and young, noble and ignoble, of hardship and injury and oppression in every house from these ruthless, wrathful, foreign, purely pagan people."[5]

Of more interest here, however, is the way it consistently differentiates between various groups of these invaders: "Black Foreigners" are not the same as "White Foreigners", although both are a plague upon the Irish in their own way. Opinion as to the veracity of this Annal varies: some take it as a valid recording of material from earlier, now lost, originals, whilst others, such as Brondstedt and Rosedahl, regard it as a late (twelfth or thirteenth century in its present form), and unreliable, piece of contemporary propaganda. However, having looked at the version presented by the University College of Cork as part of their Corpus of Electronic Texts project, I am inclined to suggest that, whatever the dating of the surviving text, the amount of detail it displays regarding events, people and places suggests a near-contemporary date for the majority of it. It is, admittedly, probably only reliable from the point at which it reverts to standard dating (the earlier sections are dated from either the Biblical Creation or Flood!), but from there on in, its precision is remarkable. Whilst seemingly preoccupied with the deaths of abbots and kings of the Irish, it records tension, and then fighting, between "Finnghoill" (light foreigners) and "Dubhgoill" (dark/black foreigners) in the years 849 and 850. Whatever the reason for the coining of such terms in the first place, those terms most certainly do not relate to physical attributes. Ireland was never invaded by Africans in the ninth century! The "black" foreigners appear to be Danish incomers, whilst the "white" are Norwegian. Very often they are fighting each other as much as the Irish, and under 908, it records a battle involving a force of "foreigners" from Ireland - but this battle is fought in England[6]. Whilst the Four Masters gives no more precise details, the dating would be enough to suggest at least a possible connection to Ingimund's alleged attempt on Chester.

This distinction shown in the Four Masters between various groups of peoples becomes important when we return to the Annals of Ulster, for there is an interesting, and possibly important, variation between the Annals and the Three Fragments. The latter describes the expelled people of Dublin as "Norsemen"; the Ulster Annals specifically call them "heathens". And of the two, the pedigree of the Annals of Ulster is generally regarded as impeccable, whilst, as we have seen, the Fragments are dubious at best.

If, then, we accept that the Annals of Ulster are a continuation of a proven track record within the Irish records as a whole, of meticulous attention to detail, then what we are seeing under the entries for the year 902 is not a simple uprising of native people against an incoming, imperialist aggressor. It is a racial matter of Irish against Norse, complicated by religious tensions, seemingly within the settlement of Dublin itself. The pagan Norse were forcibly expelled; one presumes that their Christianised fellows were permitted to stay, although this is heading rapidly into mere conjecture. What can be said with more certainty is that by the time the non-integrated Norse returned in 916, the original longphort had been abandoned, and a new settlement grew up on the site of the modern city of Dublin. From this time on, as noted earlier, the rulers of Dublin always had one eye on events and opportunities in Northern England, and this attitude helped "rehabilitate" the new Dublin back into the wider, Viking world. In the end, it did not matter really whether it was Irishmen or Norwegians who sat on Dublin's throne, for the insular, sparsely-populated interior could not provide the markets or the impetus for such a community to survive, let alone thrive as it did.

To judge from the extensive excavations carried out in various areas of the city, the new town would have looked, and probably felt, much more Irish than Nordic. The buildings were constructed in a style found, not only in other Viking ship-bases around the Irish coast (notably Waterford), but also in native sites, where no Norse influence would be expected or found[7]. Artisans produced metal and other goods, all equally acceptable in Irish, English and Norse contexts: the items were being made for an Irish Sea marketplace that stretched from the Outer Hebrides to Bristol, in the heart of Wessex[8]. The town was cramped, crowded with buildings, seemingly up to four or five on a single plot, and a degree of planning appears to have been employed when laying out at least some of the main streets.

It is important to remember, however, that this Dublin is not where Ingimund came from. His Dubhllyn, or possibly "Ath Cliath" (the name of the settlement recorded in the Annals), appears to have been located further upriver, in the districts now known as Kilmainham and Islandbridge.

Railway-building in the 19th Century altered much of the landscape around this region, but in the course of the construction, laid bare two seemingly separate cemeteries. The watercolour paintings of the artefacts recovered at the time are well-known, and many of the items themselves remain in the Museum of Ireland, for all to see. What is striking about the collection, however, is the amount of goods found in the graves: weapons and shields, women's brooches and domestic tools. Many of the swords can be matched to types known from the Scandinavian homelands, and so there can be little argument that these graves represent the deceased of the original Norse settlement on the Liffey. Furthermore, the nature of their burial reveals them to have been heathen, and thus once more the hard evidence lends weight to the words in the original sources. It can be fairly safely asserted that, when Ingimund and his followers were forced out of their longphort, the primary reason was one of religion. The fact of their being foreigners was convenient, but not essential. Other ship-bases do not appear to have been "purged" in the same way, but many post-date the founding of Dublin. Possibly there was either something extra-nasty (to Irish sensibilities) about Ingimund's brand of heathenism, or the local Christian community was itself unusually intolerant of alternative faiths. On this point, we can only postulate; both the sources and the archaeology are silent.

NOTES

[1]   I am particularly indebted to the work done by F.T. Wainwright, and his masterly presentations of his deductions, as presented in Cavill, Harding & Jesch,"Wirral and its Viking Heritage", Nottingham (EPNS), 2000. This volume presents the entirety of I.L. Foster's translation of The Three Fragments, rather than John O'Donovan's.

[2]   ibid., p.25. Wainwright cites a further source: Birch, "Cartularium Saxonicum",no.487, London, 1885-99.

[3]   see [1] above. Practically any current work touching on this subject will make reference to, but also distrust, the material in The Three Fragments. See also a website compiled by Stephen J. Murray, entitled "From Dot To Domesday", which not only uses the text of both the Annals and the Fragments, but also contains critical analyses of both sources.

[4]   At the time of writing (2004/5), information is coming to light of a possibly Norse ring-fort in the region just south of Chester and the Dee. (Mr. D. Robinson, pers. comm).

[5]   Magnus Magnussun, "Vikings!", BBC, 1992.

[6]   Annals of the Four Masters 2, as presented by UCC's Corpus of Electronic Texts
        (CELT): www.ucc.ie/celt. This site also contains the Annals of Ulster.
[7]   Magnus Magnussun, "Vikings!", BBC, 1992.
[8]   Annals of the Four Masters 2, as presented by UCC's Corpus of Electronic Texts

The Saga
Evidence

For all their peripheral position in the contemporary English sources, Wirral's Norse colonists were far more important figures in the chronicles and annals of their other neighbours, the Welsh and the Irish. Events on Wirral tended to impact more on an Irish Sea economy that was largely self-contained and self-sustaining; the western seaway up the coast of Scotland, via the Hebrides and Orkney, was a northerly extension, a buffer zone between the political aspirations of Dublin and Trondheim that had the side-effect of keeping the two regions somewhat apart.

That Dublin, and by implication the riches of the Irish Sea trade, were known to the rulers of early Norway, however, can hardly be doubted. Although generally accepted as late and unreliable sources for basing good, solid history upon, the Icelandic sagas repeatedly mention Ireland, Wales and Dublin. Many of these references centre around the battle of Clontarf in 1014, but the Saga of Orkneymen places prominent landowners at Dublin well into the twelfth century[1]. One of the most famous saga-heroes, Egill Skalla-Grimsson, is reputed to have fought at the battle of Brunanburgh - although on the side of the English[2]. By virtue of having an Irish Sea coastline, and an Irish Sea-derived population, Wirral found itself a part of this Scandinavian world far more than it was part of the newly-formed England.

By the time the Norwegian king Magnus "Barelegs" set out on an expedition designed to subjugate Dublin and its markets, however, the Viking Age in England was over. Duke William of Normandy had conquered in 1066, and had died in 1087, the result of a riding accident whilst campaigning in his old Duchy. Within ten years of his victory at Hastings, his new territory had been parcelled up and distributed among his liege-men. In 1071, Hugh Lupus got Chester and its associated shire, and to judge from surviving records, this included Wirral. In 1086, either William or his son commissioned the document that came to be known as Domesday Book; within its pages, of the fifty-one manors listed on Wirral, forty-two belonged to Chester's Earl or his tenants. Furthermore, the majority of land-holdings in what had once been a solidly Norse enclave now had masters with English, or Anglicised, names, some considerable time before such name-forms became popular or prevalent in the "Old Country"[3].

Plotting the new manorial map can be quite illuminating: most of the Earl's lands run along the Mersey shore, whilst those of his cousin, Robert of Rhuddlan, face the Dee. Between them lies a belt of smaller manors, often subdivided from larger estates, and often described as "waste" in Domesday[4]. The impression is that these two new powers in the land, Hugh and Robert, were employing Wirral as a frontier post, watching for seaborne troublemakers; the interior was of no importance or interest to them, and they had let out their manors to more "trustworthy" stock than the descendants of Ingimund might have been.

Apart from a few lame forays against the eastern coastline by various Danish rulers, and the mopping-up of patches of English dissent, England was secure under William and, as the Norman fashion for castles spread across the land, the likelihood of serious trouble must have seemed remote. Scandinavia, after three hundred years of storming across Europe, was imploding, its energies spent, and the weight of the Church pressing ever harder against the very idea of Viking exploits and their attendant chaos. Yet Magnus, for reasons that remain shrouded in mystery, decided that the time was ripe: *"...kings are made for honour, not for long life"*, according to his saga at least[5], and sometime around 1096, he assembled a fleet and set off.

The main points of his journey are described in his very own saga, which forms part of "Heimskringla", a history of the kings of Norway compiled by the Icelandic antiquarian Snorri Sturlusson. Snorri is thought to be responsible for a great number of what are now regarded as "classic" Icelandic family sagas, and it is often conceded that these are at least based on earlier, often oral, material collected by him. At the same time, it is often easy to spot where Snorri has wielded the editorial hand rather heavily, and events set in ninth- or tenth-century Iceland have a feel and a style more in keeping with the turbulent and often dangerous times of Snorri's own thirteenth century, when huge gangs of armed men roamed Iceland unchecked. Snorri himself met a violent end: having dabbled in local politics once too often, he was cornered in his own sauna and butchered.

Magnus's adventure is noted in other sources, however, and versions of his saga can be found in "Fagrskinna" and "Morkinskinna", among others. Having more than one source is always a good thing, and if they agree on major points, then even better. Thus, it can be said with some confidence that Magnus set off from Norway, and by way of Orkney (where he summarily removed the joint Earls Paul and Erlend) and the Hebrides, came into the Irish Sea. He fought the Dubliners and won, before moving on to Man and subjugating the dominant elements of the population there. In a single voyage, a foreign king had, effectively, conquered the entirety of the Irish Sea. Only the Welsh were left, and in 1098 he moved on them.

Earl Hugh could hardly stand and watch all this happening on his doorstep without at least a token intervention. His neighbour Robert's estates were centered on Rhuddlan, which, as we have seen already, occupied that curious zone just inland from the Dee that was neither wholly Welsh nor English. Robert, coincidentally, was Hugh's commander-in-chief, and may have been either a brother or a cousin[6]; family relationship or no, they both had a lot to lose, not least the continued friendship of the king in London, should this sudden threat turn towards them and disturb the peace of the realm.

It has not been possible to pinpoint Hugh's exact moves. The Anglo-Saxon Chronicles and Magnus' saga both agree, however, that their forces met on Anglesey, so the probability has to be that Hugh gathered his garrison from Chester, along with men from deeper in Cheshire, and then marched to Rhuddlan, in order to meet up with Robert and swell his army still further. Whether he commandeered men from Wirral is not known, but as he and Robert both held estates there, they would certainly have been entitled to. To judge from the evidence of the tenant names in Domesday, any friendly feelings the Wirral-men might have had towards Magnus would have been impotent, but still the Earl may have felt that their reliability might be in question when it came to the crunch.

The account of the campaign's conclusion in the Anglo-Saxon Chronicle is blunt: *"Eorl Hugo was killed in Anglesey by sea-rovers, and his brother Robert became his heir, as he had the king's consent."*[7].

King Magnus' Saga records that there were two Earl Hughs present: Hugh the Stout, and Hugh the Brave. There is no mention of a Robert, either brother or cousin, but Hugh the Stout is recorded elsewhere, under his nickname of "Gross Venor"- the big falconer - and thus the beginnings of the Grosvenor family, now Dukes of Westminster and one of the largest landowners in the country.

Hugh the Brave is recorded by the saga as being killed by an arrow from the king's hand, as is traditional and formulaic in many sagas, but given that Hugh the Stout is generally considered to have been the Earl, this must be an error in the saga. Whilst neither the English nor the Saga sources actually claim a victory for either side, the fact remains that William had to nominate a successor to the Earldom of Chester, and Magnus sailed away in triumph. He did not make any further incursion into either England or Wales, according to his saga, and so his victory may not have been a particularly easy one. What became of the other Hugh, or Robert de Rhuddlan, is not known. If they survived, they must have headed back into Wales, but given that Anglesey was - and remains - an island, such a retreat may not have been possible. They may have waited nearby until Magnus had gone before making good a retreat.

There is no direct mention of Wirral involvement in any of this business: the compiler of the Anglo-Saxon Chronicle, no doubt under close royal scrutiny, is unlikely to mention any level of revolt, more especially after

William's retaliations of 1069-70. The matter only merits attention at all because of the death of the Earl, and this is carefully ascribed to "sea-rovers", a nice, vague term that could be used to cover a multitude of possibilities. The scribe did his best, and gleaned what he could from a brief and no doubt garbled report coming into the orbit of the king. As for the saga, poetry embedded within it reveals a good knowledge of the geography of the Hebridean islands, and the main settlements on the coasts of Ireland, so if support of any significance had been forthcoming from Wirral, it is a reasonable assumption that it would have been mentioned, adding as it would to the king's fame and renown. So the likelihood is that, by the end of the eleventh century, the time of Norse-derived supremacy on Wirral was over. Very probably, it had not survived the initial Norman onslaught in the wake of Hastings, and the reprisals visited upon Chester, York and elsewhere across the North would only have served to drive home the lesson of Wirral's new, reduced status.

NOTES

[1]   Orkneyinga Saga (trans. Palsson & Edwards): Penguin, 1984
[2]   Egil's Saga (trans. Palsson & Edwards): Penguin, 1980
[3]   Randall, D. : "The Search For Old Wirral", Countyvise, 1993
[4]   ibid.
[5]   Found in "Heimskringla", Norroena Society, London, 1907. Now available via the Berkely Digital Library SunSITE (www.sunsite.org)
[6]   There is a degree of confusion: the ASC reference says Hugh's brother Robert attained the earldom on his death, whilst Stenton and others describe Robert of Rhuddlan as his cousin. It may be that Hugh had both a brother and a cousin named Robert; it was, after all, a very popular Norman name.
[7]   Savage, A. : "The Anglo-Saxon Chronicles", Guild Press, 1986

THE ROUTES OF MAGNUS BARELEGS AND
EARLS HUGH & ROBERT 1098 A.D

The escarpment at Liscard, seen from Leasowe plain. Liscard usually translates as "the hall on the rock", and if so, this is the most likely place for it to have been, commanding as it does good views both inland and out across the Irish Sea.

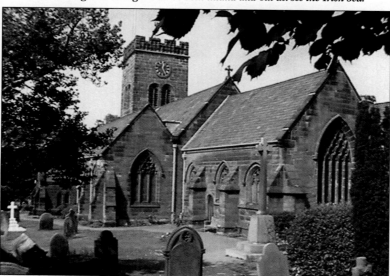

The modern church of St. Bridget, West Kirby. Although the church building does not date back to Ingimund's time, the circular enclosure around it is probably even older.

Soldier's Field, Bebington: the probable site of the battle of Brunanburgh in 936 AD. Now part of Brackenwood Golf Club.

Part of a Saxon-period wheeled cross-head, now in the fabric of Church of the Holy Cross, Woodchurch. Discovered in its original position during undated restoration work in the old Sanctuary.

The Church of the Holy Cross at Woodchurch still stands in its original circular enclosure, which, as at West Kirby, almost certainly predates the Norse incursion of 902AD. This is part of the boundary.

An ancient yew tree within the churchyard at Woodchurch, testifying to the old age of the site.

Buildings in Lower Bridge Street, Chester, showing the Viking-Age land plots. This narrow-fronted, deep style of building is found all over the Viking world.

Frontal view of St. Olav's church, Chester. The dedication of this church to St. Olav places its foundation at around 1035-1050 AD, although the current building is newer.

This building is currently a Doll Hospital, and whilst not itself dating back to Chester's "Golden Age", the plot on which it stands, does.

The remains of a Roman wall-tower: Pepper Street, Chester. This is likely to have also formed part of the Mercian defences when Aethelflaed refortified the city in 907 AD.

Twt Hill, Rhuddlan, part of the original Norman motte-and-bailey castle on the site. This mound would have overlooked the older Mercian burgh of Cledemutha.

This view of the surrounding area shows the line of at least one embankment belonging to the burgh.

The North Welsh hills, as seen from Parkgate, Wirral.

The view across Red Wharf Bay, Anglesey.

The site of the settlement at Llanbedrgoch, Anglesey.

The middle field in this view marks the site of the main settlement.
The ridge in the background is also on Anglesey.

Fighters or Farmers?

We must now turn to the matter of the type of people who comprised Ingimund's group of exiles. Wainwright concluded that "...the Norse settlement of Wirral was not a military conquest so much as a peaceful infiltration..."[1]. This opinion is based upon the observation that, on Wirral, all the village names recorded in Domesday Book can be shown as English in origin, whilst there is no indication that the Norse newcomers developed villages of their own, and "...were generally content to occupy the poorer lands left unoccupied by the English"[2]. There are a number of objections to this, whilst further arguments can be mustered to show that, far from being an enfeebled, pastoral minority, Ingimund and his men were at the top of the local pecking order, and dominated the land they came into.

Writing originally in 1948, Wainwright was denied the vast amount of evidence that has been uncovered since then to illuminate everyday life in the homelands of the Vikings. What has been uncovered in Norway, Denmark, Sweden and Iceland, in other words throughout the ancestral Viking territories, is clear archaeological proof that the indigenous Norse did not, as a rule, develop urban living to any great extent. A few towns did exist: Nidaros, later Trondheim in Norway, Birka in Sweden, and Hedeby in Denmark. But these were developments of earlier, seasonal market-places that became larger and more permanent as a direct result of royal intervention and interest. Outside these specialist centres there is very little to suggest that the Scandinavians cared for nucleated village life; instead, the pattern appears to have consisted of larger or smaller family farmsteads, often appearing as a cluster of related buildings, and often changing over time as fashions and uses altered[3]. So the failure to discover Viking villages on Wirral should come as no surprise; rather, we should be examining what few clues there are for traces of this more isolated, introverted lifestyle. There are suggestions that this pattern existed in Wirral: Liscard is generally considered to mean "the hall on the rock", whilst virtually all the "-ton"s and "by"s reflect a culture built around individuals occupying their own land and farmsteads[4].

The coastal settlements founded by the Norse in Ireland, however, are a different kettle of fish altogether. Dublin, Limerick, Wexford and Cork, to name but four, all began life as "longphorts", or fortified winter ship-bases, for crews of raiders who chose to remain where they were instead of facing the long voyage home in worsening weather. Thus, they have their origins in servicing the needs of a warrior elite, and whilst there is a gap of some sixty years or so between the generally accepted foundation of Dublin and the expulsion of Ingimund and his followers, it could be argued that this is not really time enough to radically alter the nature of the place - especially when all the other longphorts appear to have been carrying on much as they always had. So, whilst we might expect to find evidence of rural, agriculture-based village life among any Mercian population of Wirral, in the first wave of Norse incursion at least we would expect to find a preponderance of solidly military men, with long experience and high levels of war-skill to back up their "request" for land.

There is further evidence for an initially military presence coming from Dublin. As noted when examining the admittedly meagre sources from Wales, there is a single line in the Annals Cambrae, which reads "Igmund came to Mona and took Maes Osfeilion", dated to 902. "Mona" is generally considered to refer to either Anglesey or Snowdonia, and so we have a record of a Norse-named leader making military incursions along the North Welsh coast, in the very year that another similarly Norse-named leader is recorded, from an entirely separate Irish source, as making a military incursion on the other side of the Dee. The likelihood of these two incidents reporting two separate campaigns is, in all honesty, minimal; we must, surely, be dealing with a single expedition, led by a single man, heading out of Dublin and attacking along the Welsh coast before making landfall on Wirral and presenting himself before Mercian royalty at Chester. These are not the acts of a tradesman, a craftsman or a peasant farmer: this is the sort of action that could only come from a Viking warlord at the head of an experienced and capable army.

The Mercian response to Ingimund's somewhat sudden arrival on their doorstep is equally revealing: they capitulated to the newcomer's requests. None of the contemporary sources, be they English, Welsh or Irish, give any suggestion of resistance or reluctance on the part of the Mercian nobility when this Norse invader, for that is surely what he was, effectively intercepted them at Chester and made demands for territory. For Aethelflaed, the Lady of the Mercians and daughter of Alfred "the Great" of Wessex, Ingimund must have seemed like that earlier Viking menace, Guthrum the Dane, who had fought her father to a standstill and forced him to look for peace - albeit on Alfred's terms. Guthrum's relentless pressure on Wessex had pushed the kingdom into some dire and desperate moments, including, for Alfred, a period on the run, a fugitive within his own realm. Now she faced a similar prospect; her husband, the nominal king, was in the final years of an advanced and debilitating illness, whilst to the east, her brother was coming to grips with the Nordic legacy of the Danelaw. As noted earlier, it was only ten years before that a Danish army had been able to cross England practically unopposed, and take refuge in a Chester that, according to Wessex's chroniclers, was "deserted". It all rather suggests an inability on the part of the Mercians to offer any effective solution to repeated Viking attacks, even with help available from Wessex, and it may be that Aethelflaed, being all too aware of this weakness, chose not to put her realm in any further danger - again, not a response likely to be seen were she faced with a shipload of poor, dispossessed agriculturalists. The threat, real or otherwise, seems to have appeared genuine enough to warrant a policy of appeasement - and, as is usual with such policies, the wolf was only satisfied for a little while.

"Afterwards," we are told in The Three Fragments, "Hingamund came to the leaders of the Norsemen and the Danes; he made a great complaint in their presence...and that it was right for them to seize Chester and to possess it with its wealth and its lands"[5]. Here again, we are confronted with behaviour totally unthinkable to a group of peasant farmers; moreover, coming as it does from a source generally considered unreliable, and containing as it does verbatim reports of allegedly secret meetings to plot the attack on Chester, we do have to tread carefully. Alone, the Three Fragments cannot be admitted as serious evidence for military action subsequent to Ingimund's arrival in Wirral; happily, it does not stand alone. As with the Annals Cambrae quoted earlier, there is a single line in another source that corroborates the Irish claim. The Anglo-Saxon Chronicle entry under the year 907 reads, "Chester was restored"[6], and whether this describes a rebuilding of the city, or its succour by Mercian or Wessex forces following Ingimund's attack, clearly enough had been happening to make its restoration notable to the chronicler. Within five years of their arrival, then, these Norsemen were sufficient threat to warrant the refortification of Chester, and the planning of further fortresses in the region. It is unlikely in the extreme that this power was derived from local resources, or was this sudden in its appearance.

The Norse strength in the Wirral persisted. In 936, the English king Athelstan found himself facing an unholy alliance of Norse-Irish, Welsh, and Strathclydesmen, as the lords of Dublin continued a long-cherished dream of forging an east-west axis between York and the Irish Sea. As noted elsewhere, this dream was repeatedly doomed to failure, and this occasion was no exception. The only references we have to the pivotal event are a poem inserted into the text of the Anglo-Saxon Chronicle, in which the defeat of the coalition is presented in fairly standard terms, and a passage in Egils Saga Skallagrimsson, in which the eponymous Icelandic hero and his brother both take part in the battle - on the English side, acting as mercenary leaders. The location of the battle is given in the Chronicle as "Brunnanburgh", and the evidence is gradually coming down more and more in favour of Bromborough, on the Mersey shore of the Wirral.

Accepting for the moment that this identification is correct, the siting of such a major battle - and it must have been a huge affair by the standards of the time - well within the Norse enclave raises two interesting, and usually unaddressed, questions: firstly, whose side did the Wirral men take in the battle, and secondly, what happened afterwards?

On the basis of the evidence available to us, the first question cannot be answered with any certainty. Those who have in the past suggested that the Wirral Norse were peaceable farming folk might claim that such men would not have joined the fight at all, on either side, but as we have already shown, this argument is surely in error. Moreover, there are other indications, not directly connected to the peninsula, that point to continued activity connected with events in Dublin[7]. So, although it cannot be proved, my own feeling is that Wirral became the coalition's staging-post, actively supported by a local warrior elite with scores to settle and a bigger picture firmly in their minds.

The second question is rather more interesting. The Brunanburgh poem describes the battle in pretty stock language, applicable to any battle; but it then describes how Athelstan sent the coalition parties back to their kingdoms in defeat - so his victory was far from total. But it makes no mention of reprisals against the local population. Is this because the king had other business to attend to, or because the local militia was powerful enough to give him pause for thought? The Chronicle is not averse to recording acts of reprisal: not only is William's ravaging of the north put down in some detail, but closer to the events of Brunanburgh are Eadred's acts of vengeance against the Northumbrians from 948-54, after they had rejected him in favour of Eirik "Bloodaxe" Haraldsson. Again, with the evidence available, we are on shaky ground indeed, and any opinion is valid if any sort of argument can be mustered in its support. But it may not be stretching things too far if we suggest that maybe, after a hard fight that cost both sides dearly, the invading coalition began to break and run, but the local men stayed put just long enough to cover their erstwhile friend's retreat, and were impressive enough to persuade the king against meting out any punishments. Olaf returned to Dublin, bloodied and broken; Constantine returned to the lands of the Scots, battered and mourning a son. Athelstan probably returned to Winchester, paying off his surviving fyrd-men as he went, and considering it a job well enough done - but no official record went into the Chronicle. Just a poem, to leave us confusing, unclear, tantalising clues as to what really happened on Wirral all those centuries ago.

NOTES

[1] F.T. Wainwright, "Ingimund's Invasion", 1948; reprinted in Cavill, Harding & Jesch, "Wirral and its Viking Heritage", EPNS, Nottingham, 2000

[2] ibid.

[3] This is particularly well illustrated in Orkney and Shetland, as detailed by Graham-Campbell & Batey, "Vikings in Scotland: an archaeological survey", Edinburgh, 2002

[4] Paul Cavill, "Major Place Names of the Wirral: a Gazetteer", in Cavill, Harding & Jesch

[5] I.L. Foster, translated from the original Three Fragments, and reprinted in Wainright, "Ingimund's Invasion". Now reprinted in Cavill, Harding & Jesch

[6] "The Anglo-Saxon Chronicles", edited Anne Savage, Guild Publishing, 1986

[7] Especially interesting in this regard is some of the speculation regarding the famous Cuerdale Hoard, as well as many other finds in the region. See "The English Evidence" earlier in this book

Heathen or Christian?

It has long been asserted, by a number of commentators and writers, that Wirral's incoming Norse were already Christian, by virtue of their exposure to Irish religious practice. This assertion is usually based on the evidence of place-names, most notably Kirby-in-Walea, Woodchurch and West Kirby, all of which are said to derive from Old Norse "kirkju", meaning "church". Over the years, and through various writers, this idea has become rooted until it has acquired the aura of proven fact, and more recent commentators have tended to accept it without question. But it is time for a reconsideration of the evidence.

As noted elsewhere, the Irish sources are very specific in their descriptions of these Norsemen displaced from Dublin: the "Three Fragments", usually considered the least trustworthy, describes them as "Norsemen", whilst both the "War of the Irish with the Foreigners" and the generally exemplary "Annals of Ulster" both call them "heathens" - that is, specifically non-Christian. Ireland and the Irish had been solidly Christian for some centuries, practically since late Roman times; but by the time of Ingimund's expulsion in 902, Dublin itself had been in existence for barely sixty years, a Norse enclave largely isolated from the native hinterland. Moreover, his Norwegian homeland was still a pagan country, not to be convincingly Christianised until some years after the death of Olaf the Stout, later St. Olaf, in 1030. Even Denmark, generally agreed to be the first of the Viking homelands to officially convert, did not do so until 945 at the earliest. So, although Norse and Danish adventurers undoubtedly came into contact with Christians wherever they went in

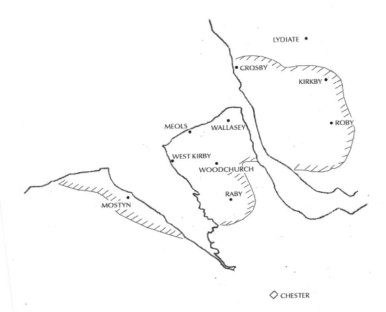

ORMSKIRK ●

LYDIATE ●

● CROSBY

KIRKBY ●

● ROBY

MEOLS WALLASEY

WEST KIRBY

WOODCHURCH

RABY

MOSTYN

◇ CHESTER

THE PROBABLE EXTENT OF NORSE INFLUENCE AROUND WIRRAL

Europe, and although they equally undoubtedly experienced unfair and perhaps extreme pressure to convert in order to integrate and be tolerated, they were, in the first instance, heathen. The evidence of the Irish sources strongly suggests that some of them at least, chose to keep their faith, and their arrival on English soil need not have affected that stance.

Turning to the matter of Wirral's "early" churches, and the place-names alleged to derive from Old Norse, the first thing to note is that the place-names themselves are not attested earlier than the late eleventh century[1]: the earliest mention of a church at the place now called West Kirby, for instance, is 1081, 180 years after the arrival of Ingimund[2]. Clearly, whoever built these churches did not arrive in 902, and nobody felt the need to construct such edifices until the time of Ingimund's far-distant descendants.

It may be, alternatively, that the Norse incomers found these churches already in place, presumably serving an existing, if small, Mercian presence in Wirral. Given the usual evidence for the formation of place-names, this is actually very probable, since no newcomers to a territory would name an area after a not-yet-extant feature, and then proceed to build it! Places are given names that reflect what the name-givers consider significant landmarks, and so in the cases of West Kirby and Kirkby-in-Walea, a church would be what they found. Presumably such structures were rare enough to make them noteworthy, and there is no evidence to suggest that the new landlords went about constructing any more. Moreover, the church of Holy Cross at Woodchurch, or Landican to be more precise, sat in a pre-Norse circular enclosure, and its place-names suggest not Irish, not Nordic, but Welsh origins! The church at West Kirby was, and is, dedicated to the Irish saint Brigid; the church that gave Kirkby-in-Walea its name no longer exists. These various elements in the puzzle suggest a small, scattered, and multi-racial population; possibly they were "fringe elements" of Mercian society, which may go some way to understanding why the ruling elite were apparently happy to grant this land to an incoming group of heathen Norsemen.

Stone sculpture has been uncovered from various locations in Wirral, notably from Hilbre and Bromborough, and has been advanced in support of the "Christian Vikings" theory[3]. The dating, however, is interesting: W.G. Collingwood, an acknowledged expert on the subject, considers none of them to have been made "...until King Knut's time..."[4], in other words no earlier than around 1020, and probably a little later on stylistic grounds[5]. Furthermore, even at this late date there is no certainty that any of it was commissioned as specifically Christian, rather than just pretty, or impressive, secular monuments. Many Scandinavians, finding themselves in a strange half-world that happily incorporated Christian myths into an existing pagan framework, could also readily accommodate images from either, or in some cases both, ideologies. The Gosforth Cross in Cumbria, and that at Middleton in Yorkshire, are two notable examples in which Heathen and Christian imagery exist on the same monument.

In short, then, there is nothing to uphold the idea that Ingimund and his followers were Christian when they arrived in Wirral; indeed, given their own cultural background, the likelihood is that they were committed heathens. They entered a backwater of the Mercian kingdom, which supported a scattered, somewhat culturally diverse, population, who had churches, and these were left largely alone; but there is no indication that the new lords in the Wirral embraced the faith of their tenants for at least another hundred years or more. For some considerable time, on the edge of Christian England, the Old Gods held sway.

NOTES

[1]   F.T. Wainwright, "Ingimund's Invasion", reprinted in Cavill, Harding & Jesch, "Wirral and its Viking Heritage", EPNS (Nottingham), 2000. Wainwright made reference within this work to the "Cheshire Sheaf", 1923, and Chester County Court Rolls (Chetham)

[2]   J. Jesch, "Scandinavian Wirral", reprinted in Cavell, Harding & Jesch (as above). Sadly, Jesch does not indicate where she obtained this date, but my suspicion would be a mention in Domesday Book, in which case the place-name itself has been transposed.

[3]   D. Randall, "The Search For Old Wirral", Countyvise, 1993. Collingwood also examines Wirral's stonework, in rather more detail (see below)

[4]   W.G. Collingwood, "Early Monuments of West Kirby", reprinted in Cavill, Harding & Jesch (as above).

[5]   ibid.

Summary

Synthesising the various sources into a cohesive, comprehensive narrative is often the hardest part of historical analysis. In this book, we have examined written reports from English, Welsh, Irish and Scandinavian sources, as well as archaeological evidence from North Wales, Lancashire and Cumbria, Ireland and Chester, and these have taken us from the ninth century to the edge of the thirteenth. Within this framework, it should now be possible to construct a "timeline" of the Norse on Wirral, highlighting key points in both time and the wider context of the Irish Sea.

It is clear from the discoveries made in Lancashire, Cheshire and Cumbria, that Norsemen were active on the English North-West coast well before the Wessex chroniclers were alerted even to the existence of the region. That this activity was in the nature of settlement, rather than sporadic and unconnected "Viking" attacks, is shown by the simple observation that most of the artefacts and sites uncovered are burials, mostly of a pagan nature, with grave goods that allow us to determine factors such as gender (although this can be ambiguous), and, more importantly perhaps, the date of the burial. At around the same time, Norsemen were being buried in Ireland, the Hebrides and Orkney, in exactly the same way, and often with markedly similar styles of personal artefacts. That all these burials relate to a more-or-less unified cultural entity covering the Irish Sea and its environs can hardly be doubted; furthermore, there are strong indications that this culture ultimately derived from the southern regions of what would soon become Norway. Whereas the Viking Age in Eastern England consisted largely of Danish intrusions and settlements, in the

North-West, the impetus was Norse. It is only archaeology and historical analysis that allow us to make this distinction; the English of the time probably neither knew nor cared that some of their "Danes" were actually Norwegians.

Although some settlement along the coasts of the North-West during the ninth century can thus hardly be denied, it should not be forgotten that, only a short way inland, lay established Saxon states, namely Mercia and Northumbria. These kingdoms were, by the ninth century, strong, independent, and more than capable of fighting wars both internal and external. Faced with the Danelaw on their eastern or southern edges, neither can have particularly welcomed a further perceived menace in the west, and this must go some way to explaining why the Norse-related evidence referred to above appears to be predominantly coastal in its locations. Alongside this postulated hostility from inland, however, must be set a reminder that such settlers may themselves have preferred a coastal location, from where they could set sail into the Irish Sea and access the markets of Ireland, Scotland and Wessex.

If this scenario is accurate, then we have a time, towards the end of the ninth century, when Norsemen settled on the western edges of Mercia and, in small numbers, were to a degree tolerated. Mercia at this time also included that large portion of what is now North Wales, and, as we have seen, there are traces of Norse activity in this equally marginal area. It is only in the ten years that surround the turning of the century that this picture is markedly altered, and without these events, life might have gone on in the same way for who knows how long.

The world was on the move, however. As the ninth century drew to its close, an army probably best described as Danish Vikings crossed the width of England in a rapid forced march, gaining Chester before their pursuers could catch them. They had already fallen foul of an army probably out of Wessex, and from that defeat in Shropshire, they had gone to a base on the East Coast, and thence across country. Clearly, they felt they would be better off in the West, and had high hopes of easy pickings from the Mercians, in some disarray as their king Aethelred sickened and his wife Aethelflaed took over the day-to-day running of the kingdom. Chester, it is clear, was considered "deserted" by chroniclers in Wessex, but enough of its Roman strength remained for the invaders to shelter within it. Their pursuers dispersed within days, and after a brief foray into Wales, the Danes appear to have departed as well, leaving only the supposition that they had known Chester existed, and where it was, and that it was a good place to shelter unmolested.

Barely had these Danish troops left, however, than Irish natives rose up against the Norsemen of Dublin, and were successful in expelling at least some sections of the population. Whether the Irish had word of the repulsion of the Danish force from Chester can never be known, but their timing was impeccable from a historical standpoint. Mercia was still in no position to deal with further threats, and Wessex, for whatever reason, appears to have been unwilling to intervene on this occasion. The result was a deal, an echo of Alfred's treaty with the Danes of his own generation, whereby the incoming Norse, under a leader called Ingimund, were granted lands on the Cheshire plain. These lands soon expanded to include the far end of Wirral, but strangely, the Mercians seem to have remained in control of the lands in south-eastern Wirral, and effectively divided the new lands from the original gifting. It may well be that Ingimund and his immediate cronies took the better lands closer to Chester, and left the freemen and farmers in the Wirral to do the best they could; in any event, his tenure of the Cheshire plain appears to have come to an abrupt end after he mounted an attack on Chester itself around 907. This was a failure; once the initial danger was over, Aethelflaed reinforced the city, and the Norse appear to have been concentrated at the far end of the peninsula, on the far side of the English buffer zone.

The Mercian strategy appears to have been one of isolating their new and somewhat unwelcome neighbours: it significantly failed, mainly because of a complete difference in outlook. The Mercians were insular, inward-looking, and concentrated their attention on events further within England. Aethelflaed joined her brother in a programme of reconquest and fortification within the Danelaw; meanwhile, the Wirral-men found support and friends across the ocean. In the next few years at least one major Viking incursion made its way into Cheshire, and it is hard to believe that the Wirral men knew nothing of it. Coin hoards were buried in Chester, and, sometime within this period, the Cuerdale Hoard was left in a riverbank in Lancashire. If, as is commonly thought, this huge mass of silver represents the funding for an attempt to recapture Dublin, then once again it would be difficult to accept ignorance of such events within Wirral, most of whose inhabitants, after all, had been driven from that very town.

Aethelflaed, the Lady of the Mercians, died; the crown passed, it would seem, to her brother, already king of both Wessex and East Anglia. England was being born, and it found its first real expression in Athelstan. Raised in Mercia under Aethelred and Aethelflaed, he is the first king who can be considered seriously as a king of England, ruling over a united and single political entity. During his reign, it is clear that Wirral's leaders thought their best interests lay elsewhere, as in 936 or 7, the Norse enclave appears to have become the meeting-place for a host of disparate elements, united only in their disaffection with Athelstan. From Ireland came Norsemen, looking to re-establish a direct axis of power between Dublin and York that may never have actually existed; from Strathclyde came "Welsh", in other words "British" (as opposed to English), but in actuality the descendants of long-resettled Irish. Their concern was mainly the northward growth of this new England, which was rapidly overtaking the old Northumbria and marching beyond its borders. From Wales, more precisely the northern kingdom of Gwynedd, came what we would now describe as "Welsh", who had old grievances with Mercia and saw little in the new order to suggest that very much would change to their advantage. Add in minority elements of disgruntled Mercian and Northumbrian Saxons, worried merchants and an expatriate Norse community left much to its own devices, and we have a fairly accurate cross-section of the forces that gathered against this new king with his new ideas. Although the battlefield of Brunanburgh has never been positively identified, the case for Bromborough, on the Mersey shore of the Wirral, is growing. The rag-tag alliance was defeated; the survivors ran for home, wherever that happened to be. The only reference to the battle is a single poem, preserved within the Anglo-Saxon Chronicles, and its author assumes the defeated parties headed for Dublin. Certainly it cannot be doubted that Athelstan won the day, although according to Icelandic sources, he too needed the help of Norsemen to achieve it. With his victory came the end of any hopes for a corridor of Scandinavian power running from York to Dublin; England turned its attention back to the eastern seaboard, on which the Danes continued to prey, and Wirral turned back towards the Irish Sea and its connections further afield. Times continued to be troubled, however; hoards continued to be buried in and around Chester, and in 975 Edgar, the new king, felt it prudent to visit the city after his coronation in Bath and receive homage from a number of local princes or tributary kings. The list of names, and the form of this homage, have been embellished over the intervening years, to the point where nothing can be certain any more. Yet the names on the list still bear distinctive forms: some Welsh, some Scots or Irish, and some possibly Norse.

The first Millennium came and went; the notorious Aethelred "Unraed" appears to have left the region alone, besieged as he was by enemies closer to home. There are local legends relating to a visit by Cnut, after his taking the crown in 1017, but nothing to substantiate them. Cnut was a Dane, and probably a heathen at least in the beginning, since it can be demonstrated that for some years he quite happily had two wives. He may have felt at home in Wirral, where, similarly, the old ways may have persisted longer than is generally accepted; on the other hand, Danes and Norwegians were frequently on opposing sides in Ireland, and he may have seen such a visit as a chance to demonstrate a willingness to "start over", and hopefully earn a bit of loyalty from a community that does not appear to have held their Mercian landlords in very high regard.

Once again, the ordinary pace of life took hold; great deeds and events were things of the past, living on only in stories and the memories of old men. The defeat of Harald Hardrada at Stamford Bridge, and the subsequent defeat of Harold Godwinsson at Hastings, do not appear to have touched Wirral or Cheshire directly, although the repercussions of William's victory in 1066 were soon to have an effect on the local landholdings. Not only were Norman knights and hangers-on awarded lordships as reward for their services at Hastings, but when York and other northern cities rose against William, Chester, and so presumably Cheshire and Wirral, were caught in the horrific reprisals that left huge areas abandoned and desolate.

By the time of Domesday in 1086, few if any of the pre-Conquest landlords still had their holdings, and the peninsular was divided up between Hugh of Chester, who took the Mersey shore, and Robert of Rhuddlan, who, in addition to his base on the old Mercian-Welsh border (the site of a Mercian burgh named Cledemutha), gained the Dee shore.

Wirral after the Conquest was not the same place as it had been before the Norman invasion. With high-ranking Earls resident in the area, the scope for the old independence must have been severely restricted; once the new lords took it into their heads to invade Ireland as well, trade and social contact must have suffered as a result. Wirral once more fades from the surviving records, and we can only ponder the attitudes and opinions of its inhabitants.

And then, one final time, the old glories flared up again. Long after the Viking menace had vanished from Europe, and their exploits were safely in the realms of history, a Norwegian king came, bringing fire and steel into the Irish Sea. Did he rekindle the flames of ambition in those he faced? Or did he send them, terrified, into hiding? Either way, he inflicted a series of defeats on whatever opposition he happened to come across, regardless of it being Irish, Scots, or English. Clearly, Magnus was not interested in restoring the Irish Sea to its former status; he was interested in plunder, and fame, and subjugating the remnants of a once-powerful trading sector. Control of the Irish Sea would open up safe sea-routes to southern England and its riches, or round the south coast towards France and the rest of Europe. Why Magnus saw this, and his immediate predecessors apparently did not, is a good question, and one that is not easy to answer. Magnus sailed on the eve of the twelfth century; it had been a good thirty years since Harald Sigurdsson, "Hardrada", had fallen on the outskirts of York, and although the Danish king Swein had attempted to "liberate" the Northumbrians in the meantime, his expedition was easily, almost contemptuously, brushed aside by William. Nobody expected real Vikings anymore, not even on Wirral. Their power, and indeed the social structure that had bred them in the first place, seemed broken, changed, and more in line with Continental thinking about kings and the nature of society. Magnus stands out as an aberration, a throwback to earlier days. Wirral seems to have been aware of this, although it has to be remembered that, in the absence of contemporary voices, it is easy to suppose too far.

At any rate, the Chronicles and sagas that deal with Magnus' expedition do not mention Wirral, or Chester, as having sent men to fight on either side when the Earls of Chester and Rhuddlan marched into Anglesey to try and contain Magnus. Had the Wirral-men gone over to the Norwegian, it is likely that his Saga would record the fact, as such a move would be massively good for his reputation. The English Chronicles might choose to ignore such a betrayal, but they still record that a Norman Earl was killed when the forces finally met. Magnus sailed away unmolested, only to meet his death when he foolishly returned to the scene of an earlier triumph, in Dublin. His luck had finally run out, and with his death, it might be assumed that the last vestiges of Irish Sea culture, and Wirral involvement, ran out as well.

But not so. In the John Rylands Library, in Manchester, there exists a remarkable document, a charter recording land transactions, that shows at least some Wirral folk still using Norse name-forms even as late as the end of the fifteenth century. One document is obviously not enough to claim that such practices were widespread; by the date of this particular charter, 1482, it may have been no more than a quaint family custom to call your children "-sson" or "-dottir". What it can show, however, is that at least in some corners of what had always been a remotest corner of Mercia, and then Cheshire, a memory of former glories and status lingered on.

Bibliography

Cavil, Paul; Harding, Steven; Jesch, Judith (Editors): Wirral And Its Viking Heritage. Nottingham, 2000

Edwards, : Vikings In North West England. Lancaster, 1998

Higden: Polychronicon. Published: Unknown, 1869

Hunter-Blair, Peter: Anglo-Saxon England. Cambridge, 1974

Jesch, Judith: Women In The Viking Age. Boydell, 2003

Magnussun, Magnus: Vikings! BBC, 1992

Mason: Excavations At Chester, Report 3: 26-42 Lower Bridge Street, 1974-76, The Dark Age And Saxon Periods. Chester, 1985

Norris, John (Editor): Nennius: British History And The Welsh Annals, Phillimore, 1980

Norroena Society (Editors?) Heimskringla. London, 1907

Palsson, Herman & Edwards, Paul (Translators): Egil's Saga. Penguin, 1980 Orkneyinga Saga. Penguin, 1984

Randall, D.: The Search For Old Wirral. Countyvise, 1993

Redknap, Mark: Vikings In Wales: An Archaeological Quest. NMGW, 2000

Richards, Julian: Blood Of The Vikings. Hodder & Stoughton, 2001

Savage, Anne (Editor): The Anglo-Saxon Chronicles. Guild Publishing, 1986

Stenton, Frank: Anglo-Saxon England. Oxford, 1988

Ward et. al.: Excavations At Chester, Report 7: Saxon Occupation Within The Roman Fortress. Chester, 1994

Related titles from Countyvise

Ingimund's Saga - Steve Harding - ISBN 1-901231-80-7
Softback - 222pp - A5 - £9.99

Viking Mersey - Steve Harding - ISBN 1-901231-38-8
Softback - 240pp - 210x245mm - £10